9/27/2009

Dear Ma,
Thank you so much, being such a good friend, and client.
May God Bless you always with good health, happiness, and lots of Prosperity!
Especially,
Irene F. Hughes

Memoirs of a Psychic and Astrologer

Predictions of the past, now, and the future

By Irene F. Hughes

America's Psychic and Astrologer

Edited by
Charles R. Loebbaka
with
Patricia E. Hahto, Ed.D.

Cover design by
Kevin Eatinger
www.pbase.com/kevin_eatinger_1

What Others Say About Irene Hughes

Since 1971 I have had the pleasure of having Irene Hughes on my radio and TV shows in Chicago. She has made some startling predictions that have come true. She has even forecast the many career changes I've gone through myself over the years.
Bob Sirott Former WMAQ-TV news anchor

At forty-seven I developed a seizure disorder resulting from a ruptured arterial vascular malformation in the portion of my brain that controls communication. I was a sitting judge, and notwithstanding the assurance of treating physicians, I had no confidence that the seizure activity would abate, or my memory would be restored to the point I could again perform professionally.

I offered no information except my name. Irene quickly told me that I had suffered an injury to the brain and that the seizure disability would be controlled and that I would return to the bench for a lifetime of service. I could not fathom how a complete stranger could discern this, but the fact that she did led me to believe that this lady had special insight. Within six months I returned to the bench fulltime.
Thomas L. Pullen Deputy Chief Immigration Judge (Retired)

I met Irene Hughes in 1967, shortly after she had predicted the record Chicago snowstorm in January of that year. I asked Irene for a personal reading, and she told me of major events in my future. She saw me turned toward a university; in 1982, I became director of media relations at Northwestern University. Irene and I stayed in touch over the years. She told me about major events coming up in the lives of my three sons. All of that has come to pass.
Charles Loebbaka Former Director of Media Relations Northwestern University

One of the predictions Irene made for me was in the summer of 1999 that I would be moving somewhere southwest. My husband and I had no intention of moving away from Chicago. It happened so fast we didn't know what hit us. Irene had been totally right on again. The last time I saw her she said that my deceased mother was here to say hello and then she said she heard piano playing. She was a great piano player. Thank you Irene.
Ann Corrigan Friend of the Author

To my long-time friend Irene Hughes, who successfully predicted my medical outcome from Brian Piccolo disease (testicular cancer) after my surgery and chemotherapy. Irene reassured me that I would be cancer-free and father two kids – to wit my son Michael Daniel is named after my father and my daughter Sydnee Joy is named after Joy Piccolo. My family will always honor and be eternally grateful to Brian Piccolo and his foundation. Irene Hughes will always be the most fascinating lady I ever met.
Robert Barrins Policeman Friend

Copyright © 2009 Irene F. Hughes
All rights reserved.
ISBN 1-4392-5070-7
To order additional copies, please contact us.
BookSurge
www.booksurge.com
1-866-308-6235
orders@booksurge.com

*(Photos courtesy of Irene F. Hughes
and Northwest Indiana Times)*

ACKNOWLEDGMENTS

My special thanks to my husband Bill, my children, grandchildren, and great-grandchildren for their love and support.

I am grateful to my friends Chuck Loebbaka and Pat Hahto for their special contributions in making this book a reality.

And to those friends and clients who have touched my life in so many ways throughout the years, I am blessed that you have enriched my life.

Irene F. Hughes

There are more things in heaven and earth, Horatio, than are dreamt of in your philosophy.
Shakespeare, *Hamlet*

Irene F. Hughes
America's Psychic and Astrologer

The great Chicago Blizzard hit on January 26, 1967. Everyone, including the weather forecasters, was taken by surprise. Except Irene F. Hughes. The psychic and astrologer had predicted the exact dates of the four-day storm twice – less than six months before the storm crippled Chicago.

The world came to Hughes. She was interviewed in newspapers and on radio and television, gave speeches, and won awards all over the world. She had her own radio and TV shows, wrote a book, and contributed to astrology publications. Famous people came to her for readings, and police called on her to help solve murders. Her predictions of events in the present and many years in the future established her as the most accurate psychic in the world.

Hughes' new book takes readers to the past, starting with her first psychic experience as a child in rural Tennessee and continuing through decades of amazingly accurate predictions about natural disasters, terrorism, the economy and stock market, and the death of political leaders.

All of this is chronicled in Hughes' new book, bringing readers on a fascinating trip from the past to the present to the future – with visions of tumultuous events before a new era of spirituality emerges. Her amazing story is a must read for anyone who wants to understand the past and "Know the Future Today."

CONTENTS

ONE
My Early Life

TWO
My Professional Life

THREE
A Blizzard and World Fame

FOUR
Celebrities Around the World

FIVE
Psychic Crime Buster

SIX
Seeing Death

SEVEN
Decades of Predictions

EIGHT
Economy/Medicine/Media/Education

NINE
Catastrophic Events/New Era

TEN
2010 and Horoscopes

ELEVEN
God's Plan

Memoirs of a Psychic and Astrologer

Predictions of the past, now, and the future

By Irene F. Hughes

America's Psychic and Astrologer

Memoirs of a Psychic and Astrologer

ONE

MY EARLY LIFE

From the earliest time I can remember, my father and I had made the pilgrimage to the front door of our rural Memphis farmhouse at dawn every morning to check the weather. My father, who called me Rene, said, "Well, Rene, what do you think? Is it going to rain today?" I told my father, whom I called Pipey, "Yes, Pipey, I think it's gonna rain about two o'clock this afternoon." "Well, that's what I'm thinking, too. We'd better get to the fields and see that corn before the storm breaks." Sure enough, right at two, the rains came down. Of course, we didn't get wet because, even as a young child, I could always predict what the skies would bring.

Seventh Child of a Seventh Child
My mother, Easter Bell Carter, was the seventh child of Mary Ann Bircham and Samuel Carter of Saulsbury, Tennessee. Mother married my father, Joe Finger, in 1908 after her favorite brother helped her sneak out of the house through a window and down a ladder to do it. They had twelve children. I was born in 1920 and was their seventh living child.

Saulsbury was rural and remote. When it was my turn to come into the world, my mother took a walk through the woods to get fresh water to drink and enough for the birth of a baby. She loved watching the natural spring bubble up out of the ground, which it did all spring and summer. Even in winter it pushed up through the snow to supply us with the water we needed.

It was the middle of the night, 1:30 a.m. She was obviously in labor. When she returned from the spring, she told my father to ride as fast as he dared to get the doctor, Doc Leonard, who lived about three miles away. Shortly after 3 a.m., I was born on my parents' feather mattress. I came into the world the seventh child of my mother, also a seventh child.

In those days, they always said that a seventh child had some special gift of knowing things. Maybe this is true, maybe not. But I do know I was given the gift of psychic insight. No one ever called me an oracle, but that is what I feel I have been and am. I see into the soul and what God programmed a person to do during his or her life.

When I was two, I fell seriously ill with something called the bloody flux. Many other children had the same thing around those parts, and the doctor had no cure. My mother stayed with me full-time, trying various teas like peach tree tea to help me keep up my strength. She finally decided to give me some Coca-Cola that my father got at her request. She gave me sips of it off and on all day and night. Suddenly, the bloody flux began to end. The other children who had the bloody flux all died. I was the only one who survived.

Back then my older sisters and brothers looked out for the smaller ones. I never went anywhere without two of them, William and Aubrey, being with me. My parents taught all of us to respect each other's gifts. Mine, a gift of prophecy, was no different. We valued what talents each one had – singing, acting, debating, painting, golf.

Memoirs of a Psychic and Astrologer

My mother was a loving, beautiful lady. She stood 4'6" with pure red-gold hair that hung to her knees and with a pure, unblemished, very pale complexion with Cherokee high cheekbones. She was a beauty. My father farmed and did other odd jobs as he could find them. When I was five, we moved to a little house deep in the woods near Collierville, Tennessee. The four-room house was heated only by making a fire in the fireplace, and we used oil-burning lamps for light. A well supplied us with water. Since we lived on a farm, we children were each other's best playmates. My brothers taught me to high jump, and I could pitch a fastball to them so fast that people would stop and watch me do it.

It was my father who taught us to listen when another child was speaking. We were not allowed to interrupt or make fun of one another. We often had long conversations about what each one was doing. My brothers made what we called tomwalkers. They were poles about six feet tall that had places for the feet and we walked on them. We had a lot of fun growing up.

How I Discovered My Gift

When I was four years old, my father's sister and her children arrived to spend the weekend with us. They were clambering around in the foyer and I found myself trying to escape from the noise. Something, I didn't know what at the time, drew me into the kitchen and I saw a ladder propped up into the attic. I thought I heard a voice say my name. Before I knew it, I was at the top of the ladder looking around for the voice. I didn't see anyone up there, but the voice continued. "Irene, your mind is going to be opened up and you are going to know many things. And I will be with you." I saw the face of a man. He looked like Jesus to me. Then, I found myself standing once again at the bottom of the ladder.

From that day on, all kinds of messages and pictures have been flowing into my head. I was given the gift of psychic awareness on that day. One of my first predictions came when I was still very little. It had to do with my Aunt Ada Sneed. All of a sudden, a vivid picture of her popped into my mind. Even then, my family knew that this meant something big was going to happen in the near future. My mother and my sister Rosemary drove to Arkansas to see Aunt Ada a few days later. This was the last time they saw her, because a few months later, I saw her in my mind's eye once again lying eerily still in her bed. And, sure enough, just a few days later, she passed away.

When I was in the sixth grade, I had a lovely, kind teacher who would take every opportunity to talk to me about the prophecies I made. She protected me, and often expressed her admiration for my talents. Once the teacher dropped a safety pin on the grass as she was walking, so she asked all of us to help her look for it. I found it. My psychic sense led me right to it.

We never heard of any bad students in our school. No one ever made fun of me or called me crazy or strange. They took me as I was. In seventh grade, I took the Iowa test and missed only two problems and got passed up to the ninth grade.

My Early Adult Life
At fifteen, I left home and moved to New Orleans, where I lived with my sister Anne and her husband, Dewitt Saucier. His job on a federal barge line boat took him away from

Memoirs of a Psychic and Astrologer

home for days at a time, so I kept my sister company. When I was still in my teens, one day I wrote down two names on a piece of paper. One name was "Bill" and the other, "Jack." I tore the paper in half and kept the pieces under my pillow. I knew these two names would come into my life in some important way.

It was the summer of 1941. I had asked another sister, Rosemary, and her husband, Guyton Welch, to take me to an amusement park on the shores of Lake Ponchetrain. They agreed and off we went. Before long, I spied a good-looking young soldier and urged Guyton to find a way to introduce him to me. It took some convincing, but I was determined to meet him, and Guyton, knowing I wouldn't give up until I got my way, brought the solider over to meet me.

His name was William J. Hughes II, Sergeant Hughes of the United States Army to be exact. Bill was an infantryman in the United States Army. We spent a wonderful afternoon together. I fell in love with him that day. We began seeing each other as much as we could. Then came Pearl Harbor and Bill learned that he would be shipped overseas. He left for Australia and New Guinea in March 1942.

Six months later, shortly before Thanksgiving of that year, a terrible vision woke me from my sleep. I saw Bill being stabbed by a bayonet and feared he was dead. The next morning, I called his sister, Kathryn Dornbos, who lived in Charlotte, North Carolina. She had just received a telegram about Bill from the War Department a few moments before my call.

She said that Bill had been wounded in action, stabbed in the left arm by a Japanese bayonet in hand-to-hand combat in New Guinea. The weapon had just missed his chest, and although his wound was serious, he was recovering in the hospital and the doctors felt he would be all right.

Bill had survived the attack, but our courtship flagged. He remained overseas for three years and wrote me only a handful of letters. Then one day I learned he was engaged to be married to another woman. I was heartbroken. My sister Anne tried to comfort me, but I would have none of it. Eventually, though, I softened and she convinced me to go out for dinner one night in downtown New Orleans.

Before long, a dark-haired handsome man approached our table. He introduced himself as Jack. I thought to myself that once again, my predictions had come true. First a Bill, now a Jack. Jack and I dated for a while and we were happy. But, as with Bill, the war took Jack away. He wrote me many letters from overseas. But, one day I received two letters, one from Jack and the other from his mother. Jack told me he'd undergone lung surgery and was recuperating at a hospital in Ohio, where his family lived. Jack's mother informed me that Jack was going to marry another girl.

I was devastated. I tried to keep busy, tried to mend my twice-broken heart. Living in New Orleans in the early forties, one thing we all loved was Mardi Gras. That year, I decided to join in. I became a member of the Krewe of Venus, an organization, like so many others, that staged the parades for Mardi Gras. Each krewe had its own day and parade route, and with Mardi Gras being two weeks long, there were parades all the time and much dancing in streets.

I remember being introduced to the mayor, who introduced me from his balcony to the City of New

Orleans. Then, while wearing an elaborate mask, I danced on Canal Street with Bing Crosby. He was masked, too, and crooned with the music in his own wonderful style. He told me who he was, but he didn't have to. There was no mistaking his voice. A little more than a year later, Bill came back into my life. He wrote me a letter declaring that I was the girl for him all along. He came to see me from Camp Rucker, Alabama, where he was stationed, and proposed. I happily accepted and we were married on December 23, 1945, at his sister's home in East Straudsburg, Pennsylvania.

After a honeymoon in New York, we drove to Chicago, where Bill had taken a job as an accountant with Ford Motor Company, and we settled in the Chicago area. We have lived in the southern suburbs ever since. We bought our first home in Calumet Park, Illinois, where I worked as a reporter for the Calumet Index Newspaper.

Bill and I have four children, William J. Hughes III, Karen Frances, Kathleen Laurie, and Patricia Ilene, ten grandchildren, and ten great grandchildren. When my own children were small, they asked me questions about my psychic talents like, "How did you know that?" Otherwise, I was always just a regular mom. The children all went to public schools.

Predictions for 2009 and Beyond "In 2009, eclipses will bring about sensational events in the world and particularly in the United States." *(Interview recorded by Patricia E. Hahto, Ed.D., on November 11, 2007, in Crete, Illinois)*

Irene F. Hughes

Irene and Bill Hughes

Astrology and God "Astrology is the beautiful mathematical science that God created for every one of us to know what our individual life will be like from the moment of life." *(N'Digo column January 11, 2008)*

Memoirs of a Psychic and Astrologer

TWO

MY PROFESSIONAL LIFE

The year was 1963. I was ordained in the Spiritualist Church in Chicago and had been a practicing psychic for some years, with a thriving practice at 30 West Washington in downtown Chicago since early 1960. One day, out of the blue, a man came to my office and said, "Irene Hughes, I want to talk to you about astrology." His name was Norman Arens, and he was an astrologer. Norman cast my chart and we met a few times at the Marina City apartment of he and his wife, Cecile.

He inspired me to begin to study the art and science of astrology. I studied very hard and learned it. I taught astrology at Kankakee Community College in the seventies. Norman and his second wife, Christine, taught astrology themselves for many years. They formed an astrology group. Norman has since passed away. I continued to speak to his group.

The Blizzard That Brought Me Fame
It was a hot and humid night on August 10, 1966, but I was shivering in Dale Albee's barn with several other people who were being bothered by mosquitoes. We were gathered before a midnight séance arranged by Albee, a reporter for the Fairbury Blade, a local newspaper in downstate Illinois. The gathering was to commemorate a terrible train disaster

that happened in nearby Chatsworth, Illinois, on the same date in 1887. But I was shivering and said, "The snow keeps coming down. The flakes are big and white and they just won't stop. There is a strange and terrible wind. It blows death before it as it drifts the snow into towering piles." Then the snow that I had seen stopped, and I said, "There is a ticker tape moving before me. It says 'January 26, 27, 28, 29.'" Then I repeated the dates. My chills left me, and I began to feel the warmth of the night.

Albee said to me, "Irene, we're supposed to be talking about the train wreck, not next year's weather." Now, it was time for our group to leave our meeting place in the barn and go to the site of the deadly train wreck. I said, "Well, let's get going then. It's going to rain in a little bit, and I want to be finished before it starts." It began to rain, and our host teased me that I had told him the weather would be nice today.

So we walked to the tracks, and the rain suddenly stopped. I was placed in a chair on the train trestle as hundreds of others gathered. They turned on their car lights, shone their flashlights, and held their lanterns. Two old and splintered pieces of wood were placed in my hands, and I saw a train of coaches with many sleepers and two engines. "There are two men down below the trestle setting fire to the beams," I said. "Stop them before it is too late. Please." I saw the men set fire to timbers soaked in oil.

Then, the silent crowd heard me say that I saw a train traveling at 35 miles an hour as flames climbed up the trestle. The first engine clears the trestle, but the second engine dives into the gorge below. The train cars tumble on top of each other. "The men who set the fire are robbing the dead and the dying."

As we returned to the barn, the reporter had been thinking about my blizzard prediction and asked me, "Can you stop the pictures that you get in your mind from coming?" I said, "No, only God can do that."

My prediction about the upcoming great Chicago blizzard in late January 1967 catapulted my career. I gained world renown, and people from every nation poured into my life. I traveled all over the United States and the world. I even got a blessing from Pope Paul VI. Invitations to speak came in from everywhere, from all kinds of groups – colleges, churches, and women's groups, to name just a few – and I drew tremendous crowds. I was interviewed in newspapers, appeared on radio and television shows, and had my own radio and television programs.

My Many Gifts
I have had a wonderful career and many memorable experiences using each of my God-given gifts. Like many true psychics, I am great at predicting certain things and not so great at predicting others. I have always been able to see death, weather emergencies, accidents, and major life events especially well. I can tune in to future events that will happen tomorrow, many years – even decades – into the future, and every timeframe in between. I can also recreate events that happened in the past. I have done this countless times. The event could have happened in the recent past, a murder, for example, or it could have happened many, many years ago. I can usually see events in detail clearly in my mind.

Tuning in to psychic messages happens naturally for me. Sometimes I quiet my mind and go into meditation, what psychics used to call "a trance." Other times, the messages just come without a trance being needed. When clients come to see me, I pick up psychic messages that they are unconsciously sending me.

I also am a medium. People who have passed over to the spiritual plane come to me, particularly when I am with a client. Often the clients are not consciously asking to contact their loved ones; the spirits come on their own. I do not and cannot control them.

When they appear to me, I see them clearly in my mind's eye and can describe what they are wearing, what they are doing, and what they are saying to each other and to me. Sometimes they come in groups. Sometimes they come alone.

They speak to me, usually to give me messages to pass along to their loved ones still on the physical plane. I can usually tell the client the names of the spirits because I ask the spirits who they are and they usually tell me. Sometimes a spirit will appear to me but say nothing. It's different every time.

As an astrologer, I can forecast an individual's future with a great degree of accuracy. When a new client comes to me, Irene the astrologer, the first order of business is to do a psychic reading. If a client requests an astrological reading, I cast the chart of the heavens as they appeared at the moment of their birth. It is important that the client give me the exact longitude and latitude of the place of birth and also of the time of birth to the minute. With these facts, the birth chart reveals a great deal about an individual's personality, money sense, education, family, children, pleasures, health, employment, career, friends, hopes and wishes, and much more.

Memoirs of a Psychic and Astrologer

This information is drawn onto a horoscope wheel, and this is known as the natal chart.

Once that is done, the next step is to do the transits. The transits chart the planets in the present, and the position of the planets is noted on the client's natal chart. When this is done, much is revealed.

The location of the natal planets is compared with their location in the present, and a great deal of information is generated in this way. For those new to astrology, it quickly becomes evident that one's sun sign, rising sign, and moon, while being significant indicators, are just the tip of the information iceberg. I still do charts by hand; I do all the mathematical calculations myself. No computers for me, thank you. Doing the charts by hand provides me deeper insight into the individual as I see the chart taking shape through my own handiwork. Back in 1966, I developed an instructional manual for those who want to try it themselves.

Astrology is an ancient science. The Wise Men who followed the star to find the baby Jesus knew astrology. It was a common practice in use for thousands of years. Only since the dawning of the so-called Modern Age have we fallen away from allowing this God-given gift to provide us with information to help us on our journeys through life.

In May 1970, I moved my office to the tenth floor at 500 North Michigan Avenue. I stayed there until 1999. It was from this office that I worked in person and by mail with police from many states, helping to solve murders. During those years, all sorts of people continued to come through my doors. One of my initiatives outside of psychic and astrological readings and mediumship was a healing prayer group.

Irene F. Hughes

Irene Hughes

THREE

A BLIZZARD AND WORLD FAME

Word of my prediction of a four-day January blizzard reached Chicago, and I was interviewed by Pat Bartelt, a reporter for the Community Newspapers in Chicago. I told her my prediction of the exact dates of the Chicago snowstorm. The interview was completed in November of 1966, and her column was published in early January of 1967.

By noon on January 26, the sky had darkened and snow was over my ankles. I had a speaking engagement at the University of Illinois at Navy Pier. A student drove me in his Volkswagen to my hotel on Michigan Avenue, where I had made a reservation three months earlier because I knew the blizzard would hit. When I got to the hotel, the management said they had given away my room. There was a long line of people trying to get into the lobby, where there barely was standing room. A man spoke to me and said he had a very large truck and would be happy to drive me to my girlfriend's house on the north side of Chicago. He could only get me halfway there because of the depth of the snow. My friend met me halfway, and we struggled back to her apartment.

The "great blizzard" had hit in the morning of Thursday, January 26 – two days after a record heat of 65 degrees and on a day that weather forecasters had predicted would bring four inches of snow. It kept snowing for four days, just as I had predicted, until 23 inches of snow covered Chicago and its suburbs. It was a record snowfall that stranded thousands, many in offices, schools, streets, trains, buses, and airports. An estimated 20,000 cars were abandoned on streets and expressways in Chicago.

My prediction about the great Chicago blizzard catapulted my career and brought the world to my door. After my early career as a newspaper reporter for the Calumet Index in the Chicago suburbs, now I was the one being interviewed.

I gained world renown, and people from every nation poured into my life, especially after I appeared January 30 on the WGN-AM Wally Phillips show, the most popular morning show in Chicago radio. Wally, who became a wonderful friend, would call me for five years, no matter where I went, or I would call him to do a spot on his show. It was Wally's coverage that brought me world fame. And later I was on the air with Bob Collins, who replaced Wally Phillips when he retired.

I did readings for callers on B-96 (WBBM-FM) with Joe Bohannon and Eddie Volkman, "JoBo and Eddie," from 1988 to 1998; Dan Rather called in one time to talk to me when I was on the air. I was on a WMAQ Radio show in Chicago for five years, and I became friends with Bob Sirott, who was a DJ on WLS Radio and a newscaster later on WMAQ-TV, both in Chicago. I did his very first radio show.

I appeared on Merv Griffin's television show. I told him he was going to get a divorce. He laughed and said I was right, that he was going to start the process soon. This was around 1968. Television shows that I have appeared on

Memoirs of a Psychic and Astrologer

include Phil Donahue, People Are Talking (where Oprah Winfrey started), Good Morning Chicago, and the Regis Philbin Show on KABC-TV in Los Angeles for four years. I made a prediction of the American Airlines fatal crash at O'Hare Airport in Chicago on the popular Howard Miller radio show.

Wally Phillips and Irene Hughes

In Chicago, I appeared on the Lee Phillip show on WBBM-TV, A.M. Chicago on WLS-TV, King World, the Hurley Green show on WGN-TV, and the popular Irv Kupcinet TV show. I was on the popular Don McNeill's Breakfast Club radio program that was broadcast from

Irene F. Hughes

Chicago nationwide and all over the world to American military. I had my own show on Channel 44 in Chicago in the late 1960s. I was the only psychic under contract for a television show that was searching for hidden treasure chests in an old Chicago hotel belonging to Al Capone. I said no treasure would be found, and I was right.

Outside of Chicago, I was on Kelly & Company in Detroit, the Cube Tube in Cleveland, People Are Talking in Baltimore, the Morning Show in St. Louis, and on television shows in Dallas, Houston, Boston, San Francisco, Memphis, and other cities.

I remember when I was doing a radio show from Wisconsin, so many calls came in that it knocked out the telephones. The telephone company called and complained. The General Telephone Company of Wisconsin sent a letter to radio station WYXE in Sun Prairie, complaining that calls from radio listeners had a "disastrous effect on telephone service in the Madison and Sun Prairie areas." The phone company said the hundreds of calls totally tied up two of the central offices serving thousands of Madison customers, essentially isolated the Sun Prairie telephone exchange, blocked extended area service calls from Madison to Sun Prairie, and obstructed toll calling from the outside world to Sun Prairie.

The BBC booked me as a panelist on a TV documentary, "The Titanic: A Hint of Murder." I have continued my writing career to this day. I write horoscope columns for Hermene Hartman, founder and owner of N'Digo, a weekly Chicago newspaper targeted to a black middle class Chicago community. A decade or so ago, while she was working for someone else, I told Hermene that she would own her own newspaper one day. I have written for Hermene almost as long as I have known her.

FOUR

CELEBRITIES AROUND WORLD

Bing Crosby was the first celebrity in my life, but I met with and did readings for many famous people after word of my Chicago blizzard prediction was reported by media all over the country and overseas. With that fame came requests for private readings and for speeches and appearances around the world.

Among famous people who sought my advice was the reclusive billionaire Howard Hughes (no relation). He called on me to look to the stars for help. It was 1968, and Mr. Hughes, accompanied by his accountant, came to my downtown Chicago office for a consultation and reading. Mr. Hughes came in and was wearing a white linen suit and a Panama-style hat. He sat across from me, comfortable and relaxed, with one leg over the arm of the chair.

I met Jack Benny when we were on Marty Faye's television program in Chicago. I was at the microphone finishing my spot when Jack came into the room. Marty said, "Jack is going to take the mic now." I got up from my seat and greeted Jack as he was about to enter for his appearance. He asked, "How am I?" I placed my right hand over his heart and said, "Be careful of this." He said, "You are right." A year later he died of a heart attack.

A politician friend of mine visited Pope Paul VI in 1972, and the Pope asked him if he knew Irene Hughes. The

Irene F. Hughes

politician said, "Yes, she is a friend." The Pope told him that he remembered my name as the one who predicted the great blizzard. The Pontiff then gave him a framed document that he had prepared for me with his likeness, a blessing, and a special message in Italian.

I met with the royal family in Saudi Arabia, and drew other famous clients from all over the world. One man was a major politician in Red China. He communicated through the mail with me for readings. The German General Counsel came for a reading in the 1970s. Another foreign client was a Japanese world traveler who came to me for a reading in the 1980s. He was buying up resorts in the United States. He wanted me to give him some fortunate dates and numbers of stocks because he wanted to make $5 million and would give me 10 percent of his earnings. One week later, he came back and told me my information had netted him the $5 million and asked for more psychic information. I asked for my 10 percent, and he said, "Oh, no. I can't give you 10 percent. I just can't." I ordered him out of the office, and my secretary showed him the door. I told him never to come back again. He insisted on coming back, but I refused to see him again.

I met with many political leaders at speaking engagements and other events that I attended. At the Democratic National Convention when Adlai Stevenson was nominated for President and Senator Estes Kefauver was nominated for Vice President, I had a seat in the box with the Governor of Ohio and Adlai Stevenson. I also attended the next convention when Stevenson was nominated a second time. When Jimmy Carter was running for president, I was a guest speaker at a meeting of the AFL-CIO in Chicago. He was there, and we met. He said to me, "Am I going to win this election?" I said, "You sure are!" And sure enough, he did. A year later, I was in Washington, D.C., for a luncheon. I was introduced to Senator Ted Kennedy, who was seated at a table with six women.

Irene Hughes at 1969 inauguration of Illinois Gov. Richard B. Ogilvie; his wife Dorothy; and Judge John Shonkmiller

I was invited to attend the inauguration of Illinois Governor Richard B. Ogilvie after his election in November 1968.

Irene F. Hughes

Irene Hughes with Chicago Mayor Richard J. Daley and his wife, Sis, at St. Patrick's Day in 1975

I was with Chicago Mayor Richard J. Daley and his wife, Sis, at old St. Pat's church on St. Patrick's Day in 1975. I presented them with astrological medals for their birthdays. He was a Taurus, and she was a Pisces. Their son, Richard M. Daley, is a Taurus.

I met with members of the U.S. House and Senate during nine trips to Washington, D.C., in the 1970s and later and also served on the Congressional Advisory Board, a group of laypersons that advises the American Security Council. The council presented me with a certificate of recognition for my service. In January 1989, I accepted an invitation to attend the Inauguration of President George H.W. Bush and Vice President Daniel D. Quayle. I was a guest at the Presidential Prayer breakfasts held by President Lyndon B. Johnson and President Richard Nixon. I talked several times with President Johnson, and a friend told me that President Nixon followed my predictions.

Throughout this period, I devoted time to writing for publications and wrote my book *ESPecially Irene* in 1972 (Rudolf Steiner Publications). I wrote articles for Psychic/Astrology Predictions on all of the sun signs and world predictions for the following year. And I contributed articles for the quarterly issues of True Astrology Forecast. My writing career was recognized in 1985 and 1986 by the Illinois Woman's Press Association, which honored me with its Woman of Achievement Award, and, in 1973, the association awarded me the Mate E. Palmer Award of Merit for my book *ESPecially Irene*. I was a member of that group and of the National Federation of Press Women and the Chicago Press Club. I was honored at the convention of the American Federation of Astrologers Inc.

In the 1950s and 1960s, I was invited to Duke University to be tested for a week on my psychic ability by W.G. Roll, who was working with J.B. Rhine. Roll called me to attest to my psychic abilities. Hugh Lynn Casey, a friend and son of the world prophet Edgar Cayce, attended my award ceremony held by the Illinois Society for Psychical Research. He presented me with the society's "Best Psychic" award.

During this period, I traveled the world to teach, deliver speeches, give psychic readings, be interviewed by media, and work with police in Great Britain, Ireland, Canada, and Haiti. I attended the Spiritual Frontiers

Irene F. Hughes

Fellowship conventions and spoke to the group several times. I appeared at thousands of events held by clubs, police groups, and political and other organizations, including the National Sheriffs Association, Lawyers Shrine Club of Medinah Temple, City of Chicago Police Department, the Midwest Psychic Fair, and Township Officials of Illinois, to name just a few.

I received keys to the city from Mayor Eddie Anderson of Love's Park, Illinois, and from Mayor Robert W. McGaw of Rockford, Illinois. There was a university astrology group in Washington State, to which I offered 500 copies of my astrology books. The president of the university came to my home to get the books.

I was listed in Parents magazine as one of the top ten psychics in America and provided a year's worth of predictions to the National Enquirer for 10 years.

Prediction for Celebrities 2009 and Beyond
Prince William will be king and do good work, an excellent king. He will be the last king of England. He will live a long life and have at least two children. Prince Harry will have a happy life. His life will be elegant, the epitome of royalty in the family. He will marry and have two children. *(Interview recorded by Patricia E. Hahto, Ed.D., on November 11, 2007, in Crete, Illinois)*

FIVE

PSYCHIC CRIME BUSTER

I worked with police in helping to solve murder cases for more than 22 years, and I have been called upon by such authorities in almost every state and three countries. I have assisted in hundreds of murder investigations. I help at no charge. In a major feature story, an Irish newspaper called me the "Psychic Crime Buster."

I usually keep my work on a case secret since police often are sensitive to public criticism of the use of psychics in crime work. Working with police, I would request photographs of the victim from detectives, and sometimes ask for clothing. I turn the photos face down, close my eyes, and touch the photos with my fingertips for an hour or so at a time, finishing in a few days.

I was called on to solve my first case in Illinois by Lt. Jerry Harmon of the Cook County Sheriff's Department. He called me for help in finding a man whose body they thought was in the Cal-Sag Canal. It was a windy cold day in March, and we stood on the banks of the canal. I told Jerry, "One shoe is missing, he's been shot in the back, and he's wearing a white shirt. Look under that rock over there." Even though the police had checked that place before, they found him – one shoe gone and a bullet hole in the back of a white shirt.

Harmon was the first Cook County police officer to use psychics in his work. He said, "When someone asks me about the use of psychics, I always tell them this story: Irene and I were working on a murder investigation in 1967, and she suddenly said, 'On April 21, I see you standing in 'the center of death with destruction all around you.'" A tornado ravaged Oak Lawn, Illinois, on that day. Harmon set up a morgue at the VFW Post in Oak Lawn and was in "the center of death."

"Certainly when a case happened we would go through the normal procedures. If everything failed, we'd give Irene a call," Harmon said. "We worked on eight or ten cases together over seven to eight years. I think she was fantastic. On one murder case in 1968 she gave us the exact name of the killer."

The chief of police in Atlanta wrote Harmon and asked him to invite me to work on the murders of the seven black children who had been killed in a crime spree in that city. About 100 "psychics" came to offer their visions on who had committed the murders. I was the only one who said that a black photographer did it. He was caught and tried later.

In another case Chicago Police called me about the murder of a young woman. I had told them where they could locate the body of the 18-year-old girl who had been killed when a brick-wielding madman crushed her skull. They gave me a sealed envelope with instructions to meditate to see if I could get impressions from its contents. I saw what had happened, describing the attractive victim and her older murderer. I gave the police a last name and an address of the suspect. They told me later that it matched the man who was in custody for the crime.

I worked with police in one case where a man had met a woman at a tavern. He had raped her, brutalized her,

Memoirs of a Psychic and Astrologer

and cut her throat. He had assaulted three women that way. One survived and was a witness against him. I gave police the name of the murderer and even sat in the court when he was being prosecuted, and I secretly gave police certain information. The man was sentenced to 100 years in prison.

While most of my assistance is conducted on a local level, I told my feelings about British Trade Commissioner James Cross and Quebec Vice-Premier and Minister of Labour Pierre Laporte, who had been kidnapped by Quebec separatists in Canada on October 10, 1970.

In nine long-distance conversations with Robert Cummings, Canadian radio broadcaster/journalist, I told his CJCI Prince George British Columbia listeners of my psychic impressions. My impression – aired on CJCI and rebroadcast on a network of 23 Canadian stations – was that Cross would be released while the cabinet minister would be found slain.

Canadian mounted policeman Ben Bertram took the information that I gave to Robert Cummings and gave it to the Canadian Police. Laporte's body was found in the trunk of a car near the St.-Hubert Airport on October 17. Police freed Cross from his captors on December 3 in a room in Montreal North. Robert Cummings was stunned. He said, "Irene Hughes was correct in both these predictions and in addition also described both the automobile used by Cross' kidnappers and the three-story duplex where Cross was held captive against his will for 60 days."

I also was asked to clear up a mystery that had baffled two police officers in a central Iowa rural town. They requested my help – unofficially – and drove me to an out-of-the-way farm where they told me they had seen strange floating lights and a large white "transparent" dog.

They said no one had believed their story, so they

had come to me in hopes of easing their troubled minds. At the farm, I immediately saw the "animal" in question and realized he was not "of flesh and blood" – what we call, for want of a better word, a "ghost." Once inside the farmhouse, I saw that it had once been used for criminal purposes. Going upstairs, I saw an old rocking chair in one of the back bedrooms. Something told me to sit in it, so I did. In a few minutes I told the off-duty policemen, "I felt that a man has been killed on the premises. I see a group of individuals hitting him with their hands and with a large two-by-four piece of wood. They dragged his body down a flight of stairs and buried it in the cellar."

I revealed during the "trance" that there was a river near the house from where I could see people unloading sacks filled with what looked like sugar. I sensed the presence of an evil man and visualized a master criminal giving orders to his men. Somehow, I recognized this person as prohibition-era gangster Al Capone. The police made a search of county records and checked with people who had lived in the area. My story was validated. Al Capone had used this house as a hideaway. There was a river on the property, now hidden by bushes and a heavy growth of trees. The sacks I saw being carried off the boat contained sugar used for bootlegging that was done in the basement of the rotting structure.

In recognition of my extensive work in helping police departments and other law enforcement officials both here and in foreign countries, I was the only psychic and astrologer asked to be the main speaker at the National Homicide Convention in San Diego. This convention, made up of district attorneys and law enforcement officials, awarded me a special citation for my work. Several police officers asked me to assist in their investigations.

SIX

SEEING DEATH

I can't tell you how many deaths I have predicted. Many hundreds, I suppose. It is one of my most powerful gifts. I am almost never wrong. But this gift comes with an important side note. As a psychic, I have been very careful over the years not to reveal too much about the death of loved ones to my clients unless I feel they can handle it. Some clients can and some just cannot.

With many of my repeat clients, some of whom are close friends, I have freely talked about coming deaths. Not only can I see death coming by using my psychic power, by examining an individual's astrology chart I can predict it as well. I do not often reveal this fact, however. Generally, I do not warn clients of their own impending deaths. It is just too much for people. I do offer a strong warning if I see an accident in their future that could be avoided. I think of astrology as a self-help tool, a way for an individual to know himself or herself.

The Kennedys

In 1961 I had a vision that President John F. Kennedy would be shot to death in his first term in office. He was draped in a white shroud, standing in a room, seeming to practice a speech. When he turned toward the door, he seemed to grab himself and crumple. I heard a shot. Then I

Irene F. Hughes

saw a man in a brown jacket, tall and slender with wavy hair. I saw President Kennedy lying on a blue rug, with blood flowing out of him.

A week before Kennedy made his fateful trip to Dallas, I told an attorney friend at lunch, "A week from today, President Kennedy will be dead." Sadly, that terrible tragedy came to pass. Several months later, JFK came through to me on the spirit plane. He said that his murderer would never be identified. He told me, "No one will ever be brought to justice. There are many involved in my death." In 1963, shortly after her husband's death, I predicted that Jackie Kennedy would marry again. I saw her with a foreigner, an older man, sort of a father figure.

In early May of 1968, I told a reporter for the Chicago Sunday American Magazine that Senator Robert Kennedy would be shot through the head on his campaign travels. I had a distinct vision of JFK standing before me, saying his brother would soon be with him. He showed me the Eternal Flame at his grave, and I saw crowds of crying people moving past a new grave. President Kennedy said his brother would be shot in the head and even gave me a time frame: "Six weeks." I told this to my friend, Iowa Governor Harold E. Hughes (no relation).

Then, on May 18 I had a vision about the assassination during a lunch with Iowa Gov. Hughes, who later became a U.S. Senator – a vision of Senator Robert Kennedy being shot in the head during his campaign. On June 5, 1968, Robert Kennedy was shot in the head at the Ambassador Hotel in Los Angeles. Hughes later wrote to me: "Certainly one of the first things I recalled on receiving the word a few minutes after Senator Kennedy's assassination was our sitting together in Joliet and your indication that the senator would be shot through the head."

I had made a prediction about Ted Kennedy on Canadian radio on June 19, 1969, at a taping for the radio program Threshold, sponsored by the Canadian Association of Broadcasters. Host Robert Cummings taped my prediction during the interview, which was attended by Brad Steiger, author of *Know the Future Today*. I said that I saw an impending tragedy for Senator Ted Kennedy that would take place on or near water. The senator would not be seriously hurt, but someone riding with him might be fatally injured.

A few weeks later, Hughes, now a U.S. senator (1969–75), invited me for lunch in the Senate dining room in Washington. I noticed that Senator Ted Kennedy was in the dining room. I couldn't help noticing that he had the most beautiful blue eyes. He came over because I wanted to tell him my prediction. I told Kennedy that he would be involved in an accident on or near water. I told him that his companion would die but that he would not be injured. He said in a calm way, "I feel my family must have a curse on it." We talked for a few moments, and he returned to the table where he was sitting. Six women were seated at Kennedy's table. One of them was Mary Jo Kopechne, 28, who was killed two weeks later on July 18 when Kennedy drove his car off a bridge into the ocean strait of Chappaquiddick, Massachusetts.

I have predicted the deaths of other famous and important people over the years. In March of 1962, I predicted that Adlai Stevenson would die on July 14, 1965. My psychic impression returned, and in February 1965 I was determined to see the former Illinois governor and two-time Democratic candidate for president, who was now

Irene F. Hughes

ambassador to the United Nations. I was in New York and asked a young friend to get me into the U.N. session, and I entered the chamber and saw Stevenson. He looked very thin and old. I was shocked. I knew that he would die on the date I predicted. Stevenson died on July 14, 1965.

In the 1970s, I did a séance in Washington D.C., at the home of Jim and Margaret Kirschner. Jim was a member of the House of Representatives and was involved in the space program. One of the guests was the daughter of the late General George Patton. Patton came through and she got a message from him.

Candy Heiress Helen Brach
Helen Brach was one of the very few clients whom I did tell about her impending death. I did her chart. Her chart showed murder. We discussed the potential of her being killed. I could see it and I told her so. But it did not help her. She had something special done in her bedroom to protect herself. She was my client from June 1967 until her death in June 1968, when she was murdered.

After her disappearance, investigators asked me to go with them to a tack store. They found that the store had dug up a big place inside the store and had laid fresh concrete there. The investigators wondered whether she was buried there. When the manager came out and asked who I was, one of the investigators told him that I was her sister from Ohio. I spent time there, but I just did not feel that she was under there. They also took me to her house. I had not told them that I had been there twice before. They showed me the pool, the grounds, everything. Before we left, I noticed a garbage can with a picture of the Mona Lisa in it. When I appeared on the Irv Kupcinet Show some time later, I sketched where I thought she was buried.

Memoirs of a Psychic and Astrologer

She had gone to the Mayo Clinic for a checkup. I told her to be careful on her way up to Minnesota. Prior to her trip, she'd had a slender mirror installed on her bedroom door so she could see someone coming toward her. Someone she knew had a key to her house. He had borrowed thousands of dollars from her and never paid her back.

On the way back from Mayo, she was murdered – beaten first and then shot. She was murdered because she wouldn't give her boyfriend money to buy an expensive horse. She told me that the cost of the horse was $350,000, and she had given him money before for other horses. She had been having an affair with this man; her husband had died and so had her uncle. She was concerned about giving this man money because he had threatened her life.

She said to me on the day before she went to Mayo, "When I come back, I want to go to Florida and stay for a little while." She never made it back. She did not give her boyfriend any money, and that's why she was murdered.

Prediction for 2009 and Beyond "I see a president and vice president being assassinated together. It is not Bush and Cheney or Obama and Biden. It is some time after that." *(Interview recorded by Patricia E. Hahto, Ed.D., on November 11, 2007, in Crete, Illinois)*

Irene F. Hughes

SEVEN

DECADES OF PREDICTIONS

Some of my predictions foresee events just a few days ahead. Some are for events that will happen in the near future. But many see far into the future. Some of my earliest predictions that I published have happened in the last several years, and others are in the news headlines in 2009. Here are just two of my published predictions made many years ago about events that have just taken place or are coming to pass soon.

• The monetary system has changed, and more is to come. We will find a "credit freeze" of some measure coming into effect, and few will be able to purchase housing or anything else. Banks will continue to have difficulties, with our government using tax dollars to hold them up.

• Better health insurance will come out, and the government may make health insurance available to those who need it. It's important for the health of the nation – spiritually, emotionally, and physically – to have a system of medical care that will be available to all who cannot afford it. *(However, the health reform plan proposed in 2009 will not improve the system. It is a bad plan. I hope it does not go through.)*

Those are just two of the current events that I foresaw long ago. Other predictions include the disasters in the government's space program.

Irene F. Hughes

My first warning about NASA's fledgling space program was made at a social gathering in Washington, D.C. I told a military friend that there would be a fire in a wiring system and three astronauts would be burned to death. On January 27, 1967, the three astronauts of Apollo 1 died of smoke inhalation when an electrical spark from a wire ignited the oxygen in their command module during a pre-flight test at a Florida launch pad.

My second prediction about major problems with NASA manned space flights was made during the flight of the Apollo 13 moon mission that launched on April 11, 1970. I was awakened from a restless sleep by sounds in my head – sounds of space ship problems and astronauts' voices. I knew that I had experienced a psychic impression of the men becoming ill. I knew they would not reach the moon, but they would return and one would be ill. I tried to reach a colonel whom I knew in Washington, D.C., but no one answered the phone. I tried to reach a second colonel whom I knew. His wife answered, and I asked her to give my warning to him. When I reached him later that evening, he assured me that he had given my impressions to NASA. I stated that I had seen a loose electric wire near a fan. Then, I saw an explosion, and that is exactly what happened. The oxygen tanks produced an explosion that caused a loss of electrical power and failure of both oxygen tanks. As we now know, the men splashed down safely, as I knew they would. I just wish that my warning had been heeded sooner.

Many of my predictions were written over many years as the featured author in a quarterly astrology book published by Jalart House, Inc., of Arizona. Many of my other long-range predictions were in my 1972 book,

Memoirs of a Psychic and Astrologer

ESPecially Irene. Here are some of them and the dates of my predictions:

• That Middle East problems would escalate in 1967 (1966).

• That the St. Louis Cardinals would win the 1967 World Series. They defeated the Boston Red Sox in seven games. (In January 2007 I said that the Cubs championship year would be 2008. The Cubs won the National League Central Division title that year.) I predict the Cubs will be sold and will move away or plan to move in 2010.

• That an earthquake would hit from St. Louis to the state lines between Kentucky and Tennessee between November 9 and November 11, 1967. Strong tremors were recorded in that region on November 9 in a 5.2 magnitude earthquake.

• That President Lyndon B. Johnson would announce his decision not to run for re-election (January 31, 1968). The president announced that decision on April 1, 1968...North Vietnamese Premier Ho Chi Minh would die during the last week of August 1969. It happened just one week later on September 3...I predicted that Vice President Spiro Agnew would resign before news leaked out that he was under investigation. He resigned on October 10, 1973...I said that Nixon would be elected president, but sticking to my original impression, said he would leave office before his term was up, broken in spirit and health. Nixon resigned August 8, 1974...I stated on July 2, 1969, that groups that staged demonstrations would diminish and disappear in 1981 "after a most unusual president has been elected and promptly assassinated..." President Reagan was shot just 69 days after taking office, but survived... In an interview with the Chicago Tribune in August 1992 prior to the presidential election, I said, "Bill Clinton will be president."...After the contested Bush-Gore election in 2000, Chicago Sun-Times columnist Michael Sneed reported: "Check it out! Astrologer Irene Hughes told N'Digo her eerily accurate election prediction in the November 2 issue, 'Before Election Night is over, one candidate will be announced as winner; then when more votes come in, it will be the other one. What a mess!'"

Here are some direct quotes from my 1972 book for predictions far into the future and the dates of predictions prior to the book's publication:

- "I predict that the government will begin an intensive campaign against all those who are guilty of polluting the air" (July 11, 1969). The Environmental Protection Agency was established to consolidate federal programs into one agency and opened its doors on December 2, 1970.
- Cars of the future will be much smaller and in different shapes from what they are now" (September 20, 1967).
- "Just imagine in five to ten years we'll be enjoying international TV – a program shown in Africa or Australia will be picked up here..." (January 17, 1968). Ted Turner launched the Cable News Network on in 1980.
- Cars will have "a means of communication installed so that an intercom call or phone call can be made to a repair station" (February 28, 1968). OnStar was introduced in 1996.

Predictions for 2009 and Beyond "From 2012 until 2024 is a time of ending of old ways of everything and a more beautiful earth being created as all the old ways end."

EIGHT

ECONOMY/MEDICINE
MEDIA/EDUCATION

Economists who are "experts" in predicting near-term and future trends in the economy and the stock market are often wrong. How many times have you heard news reports that the stock market rose higher than forecast, or unemployment fell further than expected?

What I know is that we are headed for a depression in the United States that will be worse than the one in 1929. We are going in this direction now. *(Interview recorded by Patricia E. Hahto, Ed.D., on November 11, 2007, in Crete, Illinois)*

Astrologically, when Saturn – planet of sorrows, bankruptcies, deaths – was in the nation's birth sign of Cancer for two years, it meant that Wall Street may not only change officials, but also the system and even the place of business. Our nation will need great support, rather than defiant, destructive comments and acts by its people.

My predictions for the stock market and the economy are a regular part of my annual column in N'Digo that looks ahead to the new year and the years beyond. I had seen the economic problems as long ago as 2003 when I published a prediction that we were in the beginning of a "depression" that would be in full swing before mid-2006. I stated that when Saturn enters Leo on July 16, 2005, and

Irene F. Hughes

"squares" Taurus (the planet of money, stock market, Wall Street, earth, crops, weather, death), mortgages would be more difficult to get. In my N'Digo predictions for 2006 and beyond, I stated that predictions of others that the economy was improving were wrong. We are in a massive depression, more difficult than 1929, which will last for three years.

The market is ruled by the sign Taurus. Everyone born – and everything organized, planted, birds, chickens, things of beauty – under Taurus were under the devastating "square" by Saturn. That may be why members of the media all wear black-striped, mournful 1929 (market crash, depression) clothing. I said in 2007 that at this time, Jupiter, the great planet of wealth, is transiting through Scorpio, being "squared" by Saturn. Saturn, the "bankruptcy" planet, will disturb many things worldwide until October 29, 2009.

The first events that are a prelude to this prediction are happening. Since the current recession began, millions jobs have been lost. Two-thirds of those jobs were lost between November of 2008 and April of 2009. There were a record number of 600,000 job losses in four consecutive months. Some "experts" now estimate that employment won't return to its pre-recession level until at least 2012.

Bankruptcies will continue across the whole nation. The worst market is coming, and things will go down the drain again by the fall of 2009. Oil will go up to $400 a barrel and gas up to $10 a gallon. The stock market will get worse and worse and totally collapse by 2011, and we will have a total new economic situation. There won't be a stock market. There will be some kind of card that people use for everything. Great losses of jobs will continue because of

Memoirs of a Psychic and Astrologer

bankruptcies and abandonment of homes. The promises of new jobs will not occur. There is not enough money to continue making loans to each needy company, bank, and organization.

Saturn, the planet that rules fate, death, bankruptcy, and other great losses, is in Virgo until November 29, 2009, slowing down the good to Virgo and causing the millions of bankruptcies going on now and the slowing down and crashing of the stock market. The economy will be worse than ever with Social Security ending four years earlier than previously planned and Medicaid ending two years sooner – both before 2012.

I have always been able to foresee the major influences that would affect the future of the economy and stocks. I am the only psychic astrologer who predicted the 1987 stock market crash a year before it happened – and again nine days before it occurred on October 19. I appeared at an October 10 fundraising event for a library in Glenview, Illinois. At that time I told the audience, in answer to a question from a stockbroker, "The market will go down at least 400 points before October 20."

In September, volatility had ruled the market, responding to both good and bad economic information. On October 6, the Dow suffered its largest point loss in a single day. From October 14 to 16, it fell more than 260 points. On Monday October 19, the Dow Jones fell 508 points, a 22 percent decline in value in just a single day, just as I had predicted. Investors in the stock market lost more than $500 billion that day.

Medicine

There will be implants of the brain. In the not-too-distant future, it will be possible for every organ to be transplanted. Some day it will be possible for a man's head to be transplanted. Knowledge will be gained about what the body really needs in food supplements, and medical treatments will be like miracles. Food supplements that provide the needed minerals, chemicals, energy, and rebuilding of internal body parts will become more and more the norm. The need for massive meals will be over. Insertions of "chips" that will show what needs to be healed, and those that contain healing medicines will replace the old bungling, uncomfortable use of outdated medical equipment. Mankind will eat and use health-giving foods that will provide longer life. Living beyond 100 will no longer be just a dream. These methods will keep internal organs constantly in good repair.

Medicines that have temporarily seemed to heal, but have actually been more harmful and caused deterioration to the body, will no longer be in existence. Many destructive diseases of the current times will be prevented and ended.

Breakthroughs will be made in healing hearts with stem cell material removed from the individual's legs. Strokes will be prevented and some healed. Also, I had predicted that methods to cure diabetes II especially would come about in 2006 and 2007, due to scientists doing research during the past 10 years. There will be breakthroughs during the next five years for genuine longevity, prevention and healing of Alzheimer's, prevention of and healing of strokes, paralysis, even the discovery to regain hearing, during the next five years.

The sex of babies will be chosen before they're born. This will be done by gene-splicing, and their IQ will be up 40 percent. Even the color of their skin can be chosen. DNA – ah, wonder of wonders. For example, if you have a damaged heart, physicians would send a message to genetically engineer a new heart, and exchange the cloned one for your damaged one. Cloning of new body parts will be commonplace with no reaction, like there is now with transplants.

Media

Massive changes affecting people in the media will take place in 2009, and some stations will close down. Many changes in newspapers will take place, as I predicted several times in my N'Digo columns in recent years. Some will be ended, others sold. Many magazines will leave the shelves (N'Digo 2009). Major changes in formats and ownership of publications will be marked by mass changes in employees, performers, and salaries. Massive changes in personalities, programs, and stations will continue as astrologically speaking, Uranus – major ruler of the electronic media – continues its seven-year journey, indicating total changes. It is the "awakener" of what needs to change, so that many of the so-called "mighty" will fall. Many magazines and newspapers will go by the wayside or be sold and their formats changed.

Education

Massive changes in schools will benefit some. More students will study via the Internet and in other ways at home. Teachers will need to have better education in order to teach. There will be more different types of careers due to advanced technology. Education systems will be more exciting and increase enrollments. Some of this will be due to firing of unqualified teachers and greater

Irene F. Hughes

opportunities for the good ones, with more computer classes. At the end of 2009, a lunar eclipse on December 31 opposes the sun and Mercury in Gemini and indicates a resolving of old issues. There will be lots of nervousness about writings, publishing, and expenses that could involve the death of a famous writer and the death of an important person or resignation of a political figure.

Irene Hughes at interview with Phil Potempa of Northwest Indiana Times *(Photo courtesy of Northwest Indiana Times)*

Prediction for 2009 and Beyond Predictions that the economy is improving are wrong. We are in a massive depression, more difficult than 1929, which will last for three years. *(N'Digo 2006)*

NINE

CATASTROPHIC EVENTS/ NEW ERA

"The terrorists will return to the towers in September because they are not finished with them. We will be in war in October."
(N'Digo column in September 2001, prior to 9-11)

The year 2009 will see dramatic and catastrophic events that will shake the world, including the United States. There have been effects from a solar eclipse for two years. (Effects of a solar eclipse last for two years, a lunar eclipse six months.) In 2009 a lunar eclipse on July 7 and a solar eclipse on July 21 were in the zodiac sign of Cancer – the nation's birth sign. This will affect the nation as a whole, and, in many natal charts, it is a sign that rules health and employment.

There are a total of six eclipses during 2009, two more than usual, including a solar eclipse on August 5 and a lunar eclipse on December 31 that will bring about financial upheaval, terrorism, violence, riots, beheadings, and a natural disaster. There also are four Mercury retrogrades, the most intense of all retrogrades, in 2009 instead of the usual three. Retrograde periods cause a disruption in the normal flow of a planet's energy, so expect disruption or shutting down of communication, transportation, contracts, and sales.

Irene F. Hughes

Uranus was the first planet to cross over the July 21 eclipse, the only solar eclipse of the year, and it brings strange, weird, and totally unexpected events. The eclipse indicates the President appears behind the scenes with lots of discontent on his hands and hindrance in money matters. The planet of money (Jupiter) is against him. *(Interview recorded by Patricia E. Hahto, Ed.D., on July 13, 2009)* The eclipses will influence domestic issues, purging and reform, national disputes, charges of treachery, and outrage against authority. It indicates it is not a safe time for the President and perhaps a change in his status. The July 21 eclipse could indicate the resignation of the President, or some other matter that may affect his leaving the office. The possibility of these events is significant. Obama will be a one-term president.

There was an assassination plan against President Obama in Turkey, but he avoided it. Before the 2008 election, I saw a president and vice president being assassinated together. It was not Bush and Cheney or Obama and Biden. It is some time after that. Nothing can be done to stop it.

The August 5 lunar eclipse in 13 degrees of Aquarius, which conjuncts Jupiter, will affect currency (wealth), and the December 31 lunar eclipse, 10 degrees of Cancer, will signal a time of violence, with widespread discontent and riots, much of it in Washington, D.C. People are buying guns. There will be beheadings and rebellions in the United States. I know it. I am shivering from the news.

Before 2012, there will be a series of terrorist attacks in the United States. Terrorists will attack ten different cities at the same time – New York City,

Memoirs of a Psychic and Astrologer

Washington, D.C., Phoenix, Chicago, Los Angeles, Las Vegas, Miami, Dallas, Wichita, and Atlantic City. One that keeps coming to me is Arizona. I feel they will go to hospitals and homes, and big buildings will have tremendous explosions. It will be very destructive. It will be a total surprise, and we will not be ready. They are going to slip through. It will start at night. There will be massive fires all over the country. I see much destruction going on and many homes destroyed. And then there will be floods. All of this was published in my N'Digo column in 2001, and in my 2007 column, I warned that there are enemies and terrorists within. If we do not conduct thorough inspections of boxcars leaving Mexico carrying bomb materials, illegal aliens, drugs, anthrax, and dangerous equipment, we will be attacked by terrorists.

    The New Year's Eve eclipse also will impact Australia, Canada, Egypt, France, the United Kingdom, Japan, Palestine, Russia, the United Nations, and New York City. Osama Bin Laden has organized an enormous organization. He wants to totally destroy America. He will hit anything that he can. Oil wells, water basins; he'll poison the big water basin in New York. More than that, his organization is going to use chemicals that will be put in the air that will "freeze" our brains and "paralyze" our bodies. I've felt that for a long while. I see puffs of stuff. In 2000, I wrote before the 2001 anthrax attack in the United States: "We need to prepare – with medicines that can either prevent dreaded anthrax mixed with germs of deadly disease or to help the survival rate of those exposed to biological terrorism." The anthrax terrorism killed five people and sickened 17 shortly after the 9-11 attack.

Irene F. Hughes

I have always said I know where Bin Laden is. He's right across the border in Turkey. He's been there all this time. In an N'Digo column in late 2001, I wrote that my psychic impression was that one of Bin Laden's priorities was to blow up ships leaving the Persian Gulf (Gulf of Hormuz) and the Port of Bosporus on the Black Sea that carry oil purchased in the United States. It will happen whether Bin Laden does it or has his followers do it.

By 2012, millions will be dead by terrorism, violence, natural disasters, and diseases such as the swine flu. In 2003, I wrote that this is a time of many nations involved in wars until 2012 – a time of "destruction of all of the old ways, things, events, beliefs" throughout the universe. Astrological events will shake the United States and the rest of the world until they run their course when a new era of peace and spirituality begins in 2012.

Weather/Natural Disasters
An extreme space weather event will occur on October 29, 2009. This prediction was made before research by NASA and other scientists warned that charged high-energy particles might escape the surface of the sun. If this enormous glob of plasma known as a coronal mass ejection hits the Earth's magnetic shield, it could wipe out power grids with catastrophic results, causing widespread blackouts and affecting cables that support the Internet. The most serious solar outburst occurred in 1859, disrupting telegraph networks and magnetometers.

The weather throughout 2009 and 2010 will be extremely unstable and difficult for forecasters to predict. The early parts of those years will be very cool. There will be few warm and hot days. Fall will begin early and so will bitter, cold, blustery winters. Snow will fall before Thanksgiving, and winter will continue up to April in both of those years. There will be many hurricanes in many areas. Forest fires will be set by lightning in various areas. Flooding will continue throughout the nation and elsewhere. Earthquakes in oceans and on land will be worldwide. Earthquakes will hit the Midwest, Tennessee, and Missouri. Off the coast of California, earthquakes will occur in the ocean. Uranus is going to stir up the oceans and winters with shocking and unpredictable violent, devastating storms and death dealing. Uranus rules violent lightning, the air (wind), airplanes, and airports and in sudden, unexpected and always bizarre, weird, strange ways, everything. It transited into the water sign of Pisces on March 11, 2003, for the first time in 84 years, to stay for seven years. We will have violent electrical windstorms every few weeks for all that time, wherever Pisces rules. These natural disasters will be similar to some that occurred in 2005, always in bizarre, weird, strange ways and suddenly without warning.

I don't believe in global warming. I believe we are headed more toward a freezing, not global warming. It gets hot in certain areas one year and in different areas another year. Even though some of the ice is melting, our sun is waning, and I feel it is going to be freezing some time around 2012.

Era of Spirituality Dawns in 2012

At the same time, a more beautiful, healthier, more knowledgeable, useful, and spiritual world will emerge from this destructive period. In 2012, we will live in a more peaceful and happy world. It will take a couple of years in that cycle before building, sales, and purchases of homes move up and ahead again. It will take a tremendous housecleaning of many government organizations to establish good jobs, but I predict the housecleaning will occur.

With so many old companies closing, and organizations of all kinds ending due to lack of members, this will put stress on the economy. But already many new businesses are forming and will need lots of workers who have been in training already for the new services and products. It's totally different than the old.

From 2012 until 2024 is a time of ending of old ways of everything – old systems, products, methods of teaching, exposing of evils in religion, and new ways of travel, more beautiful and futuristic everything, more enjoyable, more useful, with a cleaner and more beautiful earth being created as all the old ways end.

What is left of mankind will be more spiritually oriented and a thousand years of peace will begin. Uranus, transiting through the spiritual sign of Pisces, will continue to awaken people throughout the universe to the reality of greater spirituality, rather than religious activities. Our world will go through an apocalypse of massive changes for the better.

TEN

ECLIPSES AND YOUR HOROSCOPE

January 15, 2010. A solar eclipse indicates the marriage of royalty and the death of a prominent person in the United States. It will bring extreme activities at the Capitol that will cause lots of excitement and involve criminal and court matters. It will bring about foreign plots and accidents in shipping.

June 26, 2010. A lunar eclipse in Capricorn involves the sun, moon, Mercury, Capricorn, Pluto, Sagittarius, and another planet – seven in all. It will focus on many total changes in health and employment.

July 11, 2010. A solar eclipse occurs on this Sunday and occurs in fixed star Castor that involves wickedness, decapitation, rapes, and murders. It brings fluctuations in banks and markets. Beware these evil events.

Pluto, the planet known as the great exposer and disintegrator, is in Capricorn for the first time in 140 years and is giving out good financial opportunities and personal happiness to only four signs of the zodiac until 2024 – Taurus, Pisces, Scorpio, and Virgo. Pluto is also the planet of unlimited money.

There are some fortunate days in 2010 to use for everything you do. The ones with an asterisk are especially fortunate, with two asterisks even more fortunate.

Irene F. Hughes

January: *5, 8, 9, *12, 13, 15, *16, 18, *20, 23, 25
February: *5, 6, 9, 11, **12, 14, 15, 16, 19, 21, 24, 25, 26
March: *2, 4, 6, 9, 10, *11, 13, 14, 15, 18, *19, 27
April: 1, 2, 5, 7, 9, 10, 11, 14, 16, 17, 21
May: 2, *4, *7, *9, 11, 12, *14, 16, *18, 21, *25, *27
June: *1, *6, 8, *10, 12, *15, 17, *23, *26, *28
July: *1, *3, 5, *6, *8, 11, *12, *14, *16, *18, *20, *21, 23, 25, *28, 31
August: *2, *4, *9, 11, *13, 15, *17, 19, 22, 24, *27, *29
September: 1, *5, 7, *9, **11, *13, 16, **18, 20, *23, *25, *28
October: *2, 5, *7, 9, *10, 12, 15, 17, *20, *22, *25, 28, *29
November: *1, 4, 5, *6, *7, *9, **11, 12, 14, **16, 19, 21, 23, 26, 28
December: 2, **4, 5, 6, 7, 9, 12, 16, *18, *23, 25, 29, **31

Horoscopes for the Year

ARIES
March 20–April 19
All of 2009 and up to January 18, 2010, you will enjoy Jupiter, the great planet of wealth, making good aspects to your sun sign. All of that time will give you good financial help. You should have a good year, and, if you are not married, should find the right person in 2009 or 2010 and get married.

TAURUS
April 20–May 19
You are one of the four signs that God chose to enjoy Pluto in Capricorn, giving you good financial gains and personal happiness until the year of 2024. Venus, the goddess of love, good fortune, and ruler of all financial matters, rules you and the stock market. You will do well.

GEMINI
May 20–June 22

From September 7 to the end of the month, Mercury will be in retrograde motion. This means a worldwide violent cycle of storms, floods, fires, wars, murders, and all kinds of violent accidents. Do nothing during that cycle, as nothing ever works during it. You will be fine afterward.

CANCER
June 23–July 22

You have the moon as your ruler and have the same birth sign as the United States. Your sign rules the home, real estate, property, and matters that relate to parents. You usually love home and often like to cook and enjoy decorating your own home. You are emotional, but happy.

LEO
July 23–August 22

You are ruled by the sun, but in all of 2009 you have Jupiter opposing you up to January 18, 2010. Then Jupiter will leave Aquarius. This year there are two eclipses aspect to you to make incredible changes in all that you do. The year 2010 will be better after January 18, so relax and rejoice at the changes.

VIRGO
August 23–September 22

You are one of the four signs that God chose to receive good financial gains from Pluto in Capricorn until the year 2024. But you have had Saturn, the hand of God that rules deaths, great sorrows, and bankruptcy, in your sign that will have been there three years on October 29. Then it leaves.

Irene F. Hughes

LIBRA
September 23–October 22
Things have been slow all of 2009 for many of you, and you have Mercury retrograde in your sign September 7 through the end of the month in its cycle of worldwide violence of storms, floods, fires, murders, and all kinds of violent accidents. You will have good changes in many ways after that.

SCORPIO
October 23–November 22
You are one of the four signs that God chose to enjoy good financial gains from Pluto in Capricorn for the first time in 140 years! You will gain good financial opportunities and personal happiness to the year 2024. So enjoy all of the good fortune that will come to you in that way for so long.

SAGITTARIUS
November 23–December 22
You have Jupiter, the great planet of wealth, in good aspect to your sun sign all of 2009 up to January 18, 2010. Jupiter is your ruler, so you will benefit in many ways from it. You like animals, construction, building, and banking. After January 18, you will have Neptune in Aquarius in good aspect to you.

CAPRICORN
December 23–January 19
You have Pluto in your sign until 2024 for the first time in 140 years to give good financial gains to Taurus, Virgo, Scorpio, and Pisces all that time. You will enjoy Pluto there to also indicate total change in your life during that time. So you will also be successful in many ways and also in your gains.

Memoirs of a Psychic and Astrologer

AQUARIUS

January 20–February 19

You have Jupiter, the great planet of wealth, in your sign all of 2009 up to January 18, 2010, expanding the good fortune for you. You will change your career, have a residential move to another state, enjoy new friends, and be happy in your new lifestyle with travel and lots of fun.

PISCES

February 20–March 19

Your sign rules liquor and drugs, dreams, sleep, hypnosis, anesthesia, secrets, the black race, and the very air you breathe. You have had the planet Uranus in your sign since March 11, 2003, that brings things into being in bizarre, strange, weird ways, instantly without warning. Uranus will leave your sign May 28, 2010, and go into Aries for eight years.

Irene F. Hughes

Irene Hughes

ELEVEN

GOD'S PLAN – NOT OURS

Astrology is the beautiful mathematical science that God created for every one of us to know what our individual life will be like from the moment of life, every day, week, month, and the many years we're given. The weather, stock market, personal health, crops, travel, and wars can be charted. Your chart is a mathematical explanation of all the events – good, adverse, and challenging – that will ever occur in your life.

When you were an embryo in your mother's womb, God had given you a special day, minute, and hour to be born at a time when all of the planets, sun, moon, good North node of the moon, and adverse South node were in their special signs, houses, and places to indicate all of the events you would experience in your lifetime.

According to Genesis, the first book of the Bible, when God was creating the heavens and all that was in them and the Earth and all that was in it, God said, "I put the sun in the heavens to light the day. I put the moon in the heavens to light the night. I put the stars and the planets in the heavens to rule you, both day and night."

God created this eternal link with Him and inspired mankind to know, to enjoy his beautiful, mysterious
heavens, all the stars and bodies and planets in their special signs.

Irene F. Hughes

He inspired mankind to understand their importance, their good, positive, exciting natures, as well their adverse natures, and indicated the changes and the special timing of every event that every human being, every creature, everything in Nature would experience at their special actions and special times as the umbilical cord that would never be cut, which God created to be the link with God and His guidance to all He created, forever.

    Visualize your natal chart as a round, beautifully designed house with 12 rooms. Each room contains specially placed furniture (planets) that indicate beauty, disappointments, sorrows, all experiences that – as the same planets move from sign to sign in the heavens – would awaken the events of the "rooms" in the circular house. The individual would sense that "mystical" awakening and automatically, each time, eternally would recognize God's command and bring it about.

ESPecially Yours,

Irene F. Hughes

SIGNS OF THE ZODIAC

First Blush: Seeing Yourself in Your Sun Sign

ARIES
March 21 – April 20
Symbol: The Ram
Ruler: Mars
You strive to be first at whatever you do and take action to make it happen. After all, you're the one with the guts, the fire, and the passion to get out there and do it. You're not afraid to ram headfirst into any situation, but you are also a loyal friend and family member. Your planet is Mars, the mythological Roman god of war. Keyword: action.
TAURUS
April 21 – May 21
Symbol: The Bull
Ruler: Venus
You are strong, reliable and solid both of body and mind. You can be stubborn, but with just a dose of patience. Venus, represented by the mythological Roman goddess of love, is your planet, and it adds charm to your character and an appreciation for the finer things in life. Keyword: determination.
GEMINI
May 22 – June 21
Symbol: The Twins
Ruler: Mercury
Do you sometimes wonder how you could have feelings and ideas so opposite of one another? Your symbol, the twins, represents the back-and-forth conversation you have with yourself and others. The wheels are always turning. Since you have an adaptable mind, you use it to fit into your circumstances. Like your mythological ruler, Mercury, the messenger, you are adept at communicating your wisdom to others. Keyword: wit.

CANCER
June 22 – July 22
Symbol: The Crab
Ruler: The Moon
There's no doubt about it – you love your home and everything about it. Think of it as your shell. You love being there, getting back to it when you're away, decorating it, and having friends in it. It is the understanding person that you are that wins you these friends. Your planet is the Moon, which symbolizes your sensitivity and kindness. Keyword: empathy.

LEO
July 23 – August 21
Symbol: The Lion
Ruler: The Sun
Like the symbol of your sign, the lion, you have an aura about you that makes others want to be in your address book. Your planet is the sun, and, like the sun, you are bright and illuminate all those in your large sphere of influence. Keyword: leadership.

VIRGO
August 22 – September 23
Symbol: The Virgin
Ruler: Mercury
The virgin is ruled by Mercury, like her cousins, the twins. Like Gemini, you use your mind well. But you go further; you analyze people, situations, life. Your intuition and thirst for knowledge provide you with the key to happiness. Careful though – part of your analytical nature finds you placing judgment, for it is in your nature to be critical – both of yourself and others. But, you are flexible, adaptable, and enjoy working in a group environment. Keyword: dedication.

LIBRA
September 24 – October 23
Symbol: The Scales of Justice
Ruler: Venus

The scales of justice are also the scales of balance and this is your attitude toward life: everything in balance. You seek harmony in every aspect of your life, and, like Venus, the goddess of love herself, you care sincerely for others in your quiet, but competent way. Keyword: harmony.

SCORPIO
October 24 – November 22
Symbol: The Scorpion
Ruler: Pluto and Mars

Though a mysterious, sensual, and passionate person you may be, you keep most of your passion reigned in. You remain calm, confident, even secretive, but can deliver a focused sting when the situation calls for it. Keyword: intensity.

SAGITTARIUS
November 23 – December 22
Symbol: The Centaur
Ruler: Jupiter

Mythological Jupiter, the ruler of the universe, provides you with an idealistic and philosophic nature. Thanks to your nature, you are also fun loving and gregarious and you love a party, preferring freedom to commitment. Keyword: open-mindedness.

CAPRICORN
December 23 – January 20
Symbol: The Centaur
Ruler: Saturn

Half human, half goat, you embody great aim for a great purpose. You often hit your mark thanks to your patience and self-discipline. If a project needs organization, you do it with good humor and persistence and you don't let criticism deter you. Keyword: ambition.

AQUARIUS
January 21 – February 19
Symbol: The Water Bearer
Ruler: Uranus

Your "don't fence me in" attitude shows in your philosophy toward life. You tell it like it is. It is in your nature to take up a worthy cause, and you are sought out for your "weirdo" ways. You embody elements of the artist, philosopher, and poet. Keyword: independence.

PISCES
February 20 – March 20
Symbol: The Fish
Ruler: Neptune

Quiet, unassuming, and loyal to friends and family, you ground others with your generous acceptance of their character traits. Your thinking takes a spiritual bent, and thanks to your artistic nature and can result in creative fireworks. You understand that to get, you have to give, and you do so with a generous heart, which results in your own success. Keyword: understanding.

(By Patricia E. Hahto, Ed.D., personal friend of author Irene F. Hughes)

Astrological Terms "Bless" and "Square"

Scenario: You visit an astrologer and she tells you, "Venus and Jupiter are blessing you in your birth chart, but Mercury is squaring your Neptune." You ask yourself, "What the heck does all that mean?"

There are five basic ways that planets in your birth chart can aspect – relate to – one another. Two create positive effects for you, that is, they bless you. Two create negative effects, which means that they portend trouble, and one, which blends two planets' energies together, can go either way.

Let's paint a picture. To gain some understanding of aspects in a birth chart, imagine a circle divided into twelve parts. The circle represents our galaxy. The twelve parts represent twelve basic areas of our lives. At the moment of your birth, the planets – the sun, the moon, Mercury, Venus, Mars, Jupiter, Saturn, Uranus, Neptune, and Pluto – were located in certain positions and the astrologer locates and draws these on your birth chart.

When you measure the distance between any two of the planets, you may find they are in "aspect" to one another and therefore have an effect on you, depending in which of the twelve areas (houses) of your life they happen to be located.

Here are the main aspects and their degrees of relationship to each other:

Conjunction: The two planets are between 0 (on top of) and 8 degrees apart. This aspect can be positive or negative, depending on which planets are in aspect. It combines the energies of the two planets.

Sextile: The two planets are about 60 degrees apart – a harmonious, positive aspect that blesses your life.

Square: The two planets are about 90 degrees apart – the most negative aspect that can hit you square in the face.

Trine: The planets are about 120 degrees apart – a very beneficial aspect that blesses your life.

Opposition: The two planets are 180 degrees apart (on the exact opposite side of the birth chart). This is negative because it creates tension, like two people pulling on opposite ends of a rope.

When an astrologer reads your chart, she will say that an aspect blesses you when the two planets in question are either sextile or trine. If two planets are square, or opposing, that means difficulties. The conjunction is a little more complicated, but in general it describes a blending of the characteristics associated with each of the two planets. Sometimes these can bless you, sometimes they can square or negatively aspect you.

Learning the aspects of your birth chart and whether they bless or square you is an important way for you to identify your strengths, weaknesses, and challenges that are hard-wired from birth.

Patricia E. Hahto, Ed.D.
June 9, 2009

IRENE F. HUGHES

psychic • **astrologer** • **medium**

What Does the Future Hold for Your Personal Life or Business? Irene F. Hughes Offers You Her Unique Advising Services

Telephone Reading: $50   Speak to Irene personally for 15 minutes
   Prepay with MasterCard, Visa, American Express, money order
   Call (708) 672-7090 to schedule and make payment arrangements
   No questions about illness, pregnancy, or lost articles

In-Person Reading: $50   Visit with Irene personally for 20 minutes
   Call (708) 672-7090 to schedule and make payment arrangements

Reading Through the Mail: $50   Write to Irene for her personal advice
   Five Questions (No questions about illness, pregnancy, or lost articles)
   Cash or Money Order Only (Include self-addressed, stamped envelope; include your day, month, and year of birth and anyone you are asking about)

House Parties: $600 minimum fee Call (708) 672-7090
   Offer your friends an opportunity to meet Irene in your home for a personal reading: 10-Minute Reading: $30. 15-Minute Reading: $45. 20-Minute Reading: $60

Natal Chart: $160
   Irene will create your Natal Chart and forecast events for the next 12 months. Include your exact day, month, year, and time of birth (consult your birth certificate); place of birth (city, state, country); marital status; profession; number of children; other significant information. Cash or Money Order Only

Séance: Irene is a medium. Call for specific information.

Made in the USA